ABOVE: Uncut and uncoloured sheet of early tarot cards, Milan, c.1500. The imagery anticipates the later Marseille designs. Some features are common to other early Italian decks such as the Visconti-Sforza and D'Este decks. Cary Collection, Yale University.

First published 2024
This edition © Wooden Books Ltd 2024

Published by Wooden Books Ltd.
Glastonbury, Somerset.
www.woodenbooks.com

British Library Cataloguing in Publication Data
Labriola, N.
Tarot

A CIP catalogue record for this book
may be obtained from the British Library.

ISBN-10: 1-907155-50-3
ISBN-13: 978-1-907155-50-5

All rights reserved.
For permission to reproduce any part of this
divine little book please contact the publishers.

Designed and typeset in Glastonbury, UK.
Printed in China on FSC® certified papers by
RR Donnelley Asia Printing Solutions Ltd.

TAROT

TIMELESS SECRETS OF THE ANCIENT MIRROR

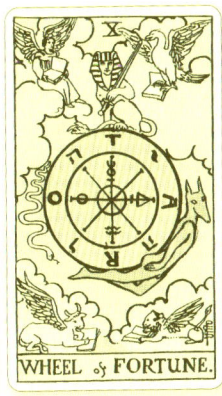

Natalie Labriola

For my daughter Cosima

Immense thanks to the Wooden Books team: John Martineau, Tihana Sare, Matt Tweed, and Cynthia Lovett. Deep gratitude to Mike Labriola and Michelle Hansel Silver. Special thank you to my husband Taylor Scruggs. I recommend books by Rachel Pollack, Mary K Greer, Paul Huson, Sallie Nichols, T Susan Chang & Jessica Dore

Tarot decks used to illustrate this book include: The Rider Waite deck (p.5 & used for the sample spreads and much of the quoted symbolism); the Marseilles deck (p.6 & p.9); the Etteilla deck (p.3); the Sola Busca deck; the Tarocco deck; and many others.

BELOW: *The great chain from God to nature and from nature to man. Illustration, 1617, by Robert Fludd, showing the macrocosm mirrored in the microcosm.*

CONTENTS

Introduction	1
The History of Tarot	2
The Major Arcana	4
The Minor Arcana	6
The Court Cards	8
A Full Deck	10
Using Tarot Cards	12
The Fool	14
The Magician	16
The High Priestess	18
The Empress	20
The Emperor	22
The Hierophant	24
The Lovers	26
The Chariot	28
Strength	30
The Hermit	32
Wheel of Fortune	34
Justice	36
The Hanged Man	38
Death	40
Temperance	42
The Devil	44
The Tower	46
The Star	48
The Moon	50
The Sun	52
Judgement	54
The World	56
Table of Correspondences	58

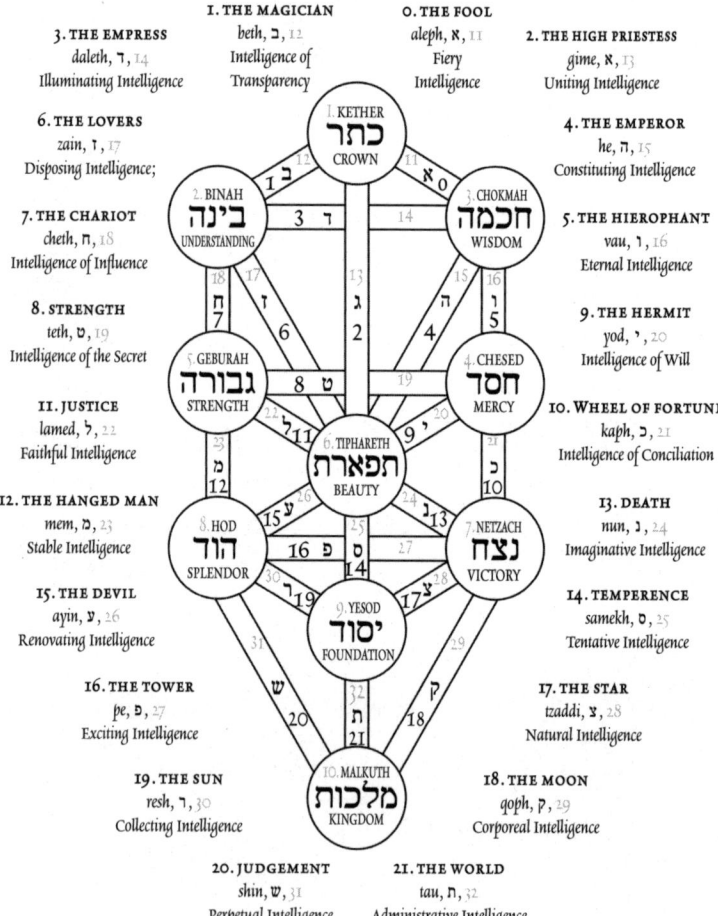

ABOVE: The Kabbalistic Tree of Life, showing the correspondences between its 22 paths and the 22 cards of the Major Arcana of the Tarot.

INTRODUCTION

THE TAROT is a complete philosophy of life. It acts as map of human nature, experience and consciousness, depicting the human soul embedded in a cosmic drama. By engaging with its evocative imagery, we form a direct line of communication to that deep part of our psyche which speaks and relates via archetypal images and symbols. The ritual of pulling a tarot card and contemplating its meaning takes us out of linear time and into mythic time, where the past and future interweave in the perpetual present, and where we can become attuned to subtle messages from both our inner world and our outer world.

A tool for divination and insight, the Tarot is comprised of 78 cards. The 22 cards of the MAJOR ARCANA depict the archetypal themes of shared human experience in a sequence known as *"the Fool's Journey"* (the Fool being the first card). This is not a linear ascent to greatness, but rather a spiraling path to wholeness that involves the reconciliation of opposing forces: rational and irrational, active control and passive release, generation and decay, independence and union, love and subjugation. The Fool's Journey can be likened to Carl Jung's concept of individuation, a process of self-actualization achieved by integrating the conscious and the unconscious aspects of psyche. The 56 cards of the MINOR ARCANA are divided into four suits of 14 cards each, and reflect the various domains of human behavoir and experience.

Tarot offers us the gift of seeing ourselves and our lives reflected back to us with clarity, of feeling connected to something larger and more mysterious than we can intellectually understand. It helps us live with the awareness that life to speaks to us through the language of archetypes and symbols, if only we take the time to listen.

The History of Tarot
from games to divination

THE EXACT ORIGINS of the tarot are uncertain, but the earliest known deck that featured the Major Arcana—the *Visconti-Sforza* tarot—was commissioned by an Italian duke as a gift for his duchess in the 1440s. Card games using playing decks resembling the ones of today were already widely used in 15th century Italy, but this particular deck was created as a work of art—the cards were larger than standard playing cards, and were hand-painted by artist Bonifaco Bembo [1447–1480] with intricate details and ornate gold leafing (*below*). Epic poems from the same period reveal that the figures of the Major Arcana were a source of inspiration for writers, and soon afterwards, the cards were being widely used to play *tarochhi*, a game similar to bridge.

Tarot was popularised as a divination tool in the late 1700s, when a Parisian wig-maker-turned-occultist named Etteilla [1738–1791] brought it to a wider audience through several books on the subject and by creating his own deck with an extended symbolism (*lower opposite*).

In the 1800s, Tarot practitioners spread their ideas through books and occult-leaning initiatory organizations, such as the Freemasons, the Theosophists, and the Hermetic Order of the Golden Dawn, who drew links between the tarot and astrology, Kabbalah, Rosicrucianism, alchemy, numerology, and other systems.

ABOVE: An uncut tarocchi sheet, block printed c.1500, from The Rosenwald collection, National Gallery of Art, Washington DC. It shows all the trumps except the Fool, plus three queens.

LEFT: Two cards from Etteilla's 1789 tarot, the first divinatory deck. Etteilla (the pseudonym of Jean-Baptistye Alliete) claimed that an Italian stranger revealed its secrets to him, spreading the idea of tarot as a mysterious body of esoteric knowledge. Around the same time, pastor-turned-occultist Antoine Court de Gebelin popularized the theory that the tarot was Ancient Egyptian in origin, and could aid in connecting to this ancient wisdom.

THE MAJOR ARCANA
the Fool's Journey

The 22 MAJOR ARCANA represent significant archetypal themes and lessons fundamental to human experience, beginning with *The Fool* and ending with *The World* (*see lower opposite*). As archetypes, they convey universal patterns, images and symbols that exist within the collective unconscious, which the Swiss psychiatrist Carl Jung [1875-1961] concieved of as a shared archive of psychic artifacts evolved throughout the course of human evolution, which form the bedrock of our psyches and instincts.

For example, the archetype of the Mother connects both to our personal mothers and also to universal concepts of Mother; so when we pull a card like *The Empress*, we consider our own mother (or children) as well as our relationship to universal themes of mothering, nurturing and our ability to care for ourselves and others.

As a tool of divination, the Tarot mirrors one's inner wisdom. The idea that the structure of the human mind is related to that of the cosmos itself, and that both may rest on a deeper universal ordering principle or metaphysical intelligence, is reflected in many spiritual traditions throughout the world: from the concept of Tao in Chinese culture, to Brahman in Hindu culture, to the Greek ideal of the Anima Mundi.

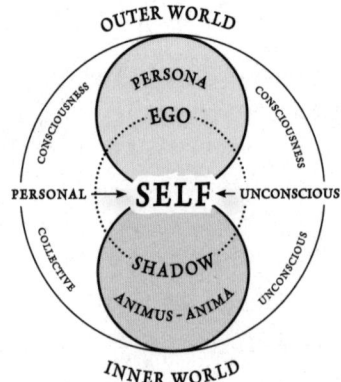

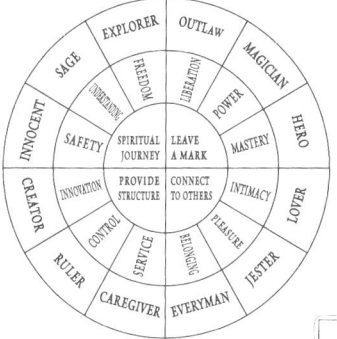

FACING PAGE: The structure of the psyche, according to Jung. The SELF is the most important archetype, representing the unity of the unconscious and conscious mind and the integration of the individual's personality. The SHADOW represents the repressed or unknown aspects of the personality that the individual finds unacceptable or uncomfortable. The ANIMA/ANIMUS is the feminine side of the male psyche (anima) or the masculine side of the female psyche (animus).

ABOVE: Carl Jung's 12 Master Archetypes, the universal mythic characters, and their various motivations. We each tend to have one dominant.

BELOW: The 22 Major Arcana of the 1909 Rider-Waite-Smith deck, created by Arthur Edward Waite and Pamela Colman Smith. This layout highlights the 3 Lines of the Major Arcana (Rachel Pollack), with the Fool standing apart.

The Minor Arcana
suits and numbers

The Minor Arcana predate the Major Arcana, and consist of four suits:

WANDS (or Staves). Fire. Life force, vitality, creativity and energy. Matters of creative realization, ambition, and personal growth.

PENTACLES (or Coins). Earth. How we use our energy in the material world. Matters related to our resources, physical health and security.

SWORDS: Air. Thoughts, communication, and mental clarity. Matters related to conflict, decision-making, and the power of the mind.

CUPS (or Goblets). Water. Emotions, intuition and connection. Matters related to relationships, love, and emotional fulfillment.

Each suit contains 14 cards, numbered Ace to 10 (*opposite*), plus four *court cards*: Page, Knight, Queen, and King (*page 8*). The 56 Minor Arcana represent four domains of daily human experience, while the 22 Major Arcana (*page 4*) represent significant life events or themes.

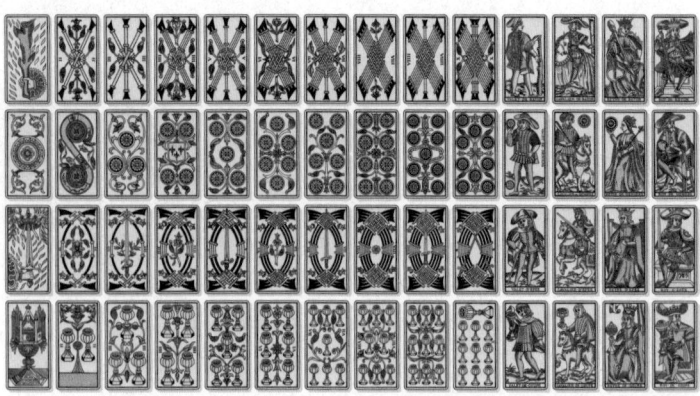

WANDS
STAVES (CLUBS) - FIRE
Energy and Action: Ambition, goals, drive, the desire to externalize inner fire through creative self-expression, managing our energy in order to keep the flame alive.

PENTACLES
COINS (DIAMONDS) - EARTH
Material Matters and Practicality: Internal and external resources, security and stability, concern with the behaviors, mindsets, and systems that support growth.

SWORDS
BLADES (SPADES) - AIR
Thoughts and Challenges: The power of mind to create clarity and insight, or to turn on itself. Mental agility, communication, managing internal and external conflicts.

CUPS
GOBLETS (HEARTS) - WATER
Emotions and Relationships: Intuition, the subconscious mind, emotional fulfillment, well-being and healing through loving relationships with self and others.

ABOVE: The Four Suits of the Minor Arcana. Each represents a different element and its corresponding domain in human behavior and experience.

1 the beginning or seed of a new chapter or venture, pure potentiality, an opportunity or blessing.

2 duality and balance, choices and decisions, partnerships, relationships.

3 creativity, growth and expansion, progress and movement, synthesis and integration.

4 foundations, order and structure, the desire to gather and stabilize, questions of fulfillment.

5 challenge, change, conflict, and instability, internal and external confrontations which spur action.

6 harmonizing, balancing, reflecting, and the establishment of peace in a time of transition.

7 assessment, evaluation, reflection, challenge, the potential for growth through inner work.

8 movement, progress, transformation through renunciation of the old

9 fruition, fulfillment, and attainment, seeing through illusions, protection, security

10 completion, endings, renewal, surrender, legacy, potential for new beginnings or start of a new cycle.

ABOVE: THE TEN NUMBERS: The essential symbolism of the numbers 1-10 in tarot. The symbolism of the four court cards is covered on the next page.

The Court Cards
page, knight, queen and king

The four court cards—PAGE, KNIGHT, QUEEN, and KING—represent various archetypal aspects and expressions of human personality. In a reading, they may indicate specific people, an aspect of self, an event or a situation. As with all Tarot cards, the context of the question will be key to discerning their meaning.

PAGES (or PRINCESSES) represent youthful curiosity and enthusiasm, the spark of a new idea, as well as the energy and naïveté required to initiate it. They represent new experiences, invitations or opportunities in the realm of creativity (*Wands*), material resources (*Pentacles/Coins*), perspectives (*Swords*) or emotions (*Cups*).

KNIGHTS represent the drive to take swift action on the ideas initiated by the Page. They embody the courage needed to take risks, but also the tendency towards hastiness and impulsivity.

QUEENS represent the archetypally mature feminine energy, associated with intuition, compassion, nurturing, and the inwardly-directed passive yin principle which magnetizes, relates, and reflects.

KINGS embody the archetypally mature masculine, associated with wise authority, experience, responsibility, and the outwardly-directed active yang principle which focuses, energizes, and leads.

For any process, the Pages can be seen as its conceptualization, the Knights as the initiatory action, the Queens as its nurturing and stabilizing, and the Kings as the stage of development and completion.

The court cards shown opposite (*and the Minor Arcana on page 6*) are taken from a 17th-century Marseilles tarot deck.

PAGE
YOUTH / CURIOSITY

KNIGHT
ACTION / DRIVE

QUEEN
NUTURE / INTUITION

KING
MASTERY / MATURITY

PAGE
OF WANDS: Enthusiasm for learning and expansion.
OF PENTACLES: Cultivating new talents.
OF SWORDS: New mindset, beliefs, and perspectives.
OF CUPS: An encounter with the creative unconscious.

KNIGHT
OF WANDS: Taking action towards ambitions.
OF PENTACLES: Slow and steady growth with patience.
OF SWORDS: Desire to speak the truth, haste.
OF CUPS: Emotional vulnerability and courage.

QUEEN
OF WANDS: Creative confidence, relational charm.
OF PENTACLES: Nurturing self and others, security.
OF SWORDS: Boundaries and clarity, decisiveness.
OF CUPS: Reflection and intuition, caring, supportive

KING
OF WANDS: Materializing creative visions, confidence
OF PENTACLES: Sustaining material abundance.
OF SWORDS: Articulating logical truth, wisdom.
OF CUPS: Emotional maturity and responsibility.

THE FULL DECK
all seventy-eight

The 22 cards of the Major Arcana (*below*) represent archetypes of human existence, major lessons of life, and fundamental themes experienced by all. The 56 cards of the four suits of the Minor Arcana (*opposite*) reflect the nuances of our everyday experiences, habits, thoughts and emotions. Together they form the 78 cards of a tarot deck.

When a Major Arcana card appears in a tarot reading, it suggests that an important archetype is at work in your psyche or your life. If a reading contains a high proportion of Major Arcana cards it generally indicates an important moment of life-changing transformation and the need to surrender to and learn from the larger forces at work.

0. THE FOOL *new beginnings, taking a leap*	1. THE MAGICIAN *willpower, creativity, manifestation*	2. THE HIGH PRIESTESS *intuition, connection with inner wisdom*	3. THE EMPRESS *nurturing, abundance, fertility, creativity*
4. THE EMPEROR *structure, stability, personal authority*	5. THE HIEROPHANT *tradition, ritual, communicating truth*	6. THE LOVERS *growth through relationships, choices*	7. THE CHARIOT *determination embarking on a quest*
8. STRENGTH *courage, compassion, inner fortitude*	9. THE HERMIT *solitude, introspection, wisdom, self-trust*	10. WHEEL OF FORTUNE *change, cycles, fate, transition*	11. JUSTICE *balance, karma, truth, objective clarity*
12. THE HANGED MAN *surrender, sacrifice, shift of perspective*	13. DEATH *endings, rebirth, transformation*	14. TEMPERANCE *blending, alchemizing, harmonizing*	15. THE DEVIL *the shadow, self- imposed limitations*
16. THE TOWER *upheaval, chaos, revelation*	17. THE STAR *connection, inspiration, healing*	18. THE MOON *the unknown, the unconscious, intuition*	19. THE SUN *vitality, joy, celebration, inner child*
20. JUDGEMENT *rebirth, renewal, personal awakening*	21. THE WORLD *completion, fulfillment, wholeness*		

THIS PAGE: *The 22 Major Arcana*
FACING PAGE: *The 56 Minor Arcana*

Suit	**WANDS**	**PENTACLES**	**SWORDS**	**CUPS**
Alt. name	BATONS	COINS	BLADES	GOBLETS
Com. name	CLUBS	DIAMONDS	SPADES	HEARTS
Element	FIRE	EARTH	AIR	WATER
Rules	SPIRIT	MATERIAL	INTELLECT	EMOTIONS
1 POTENTIAL	spark of inspiration, a new beginning	new opportunity for success/prosperity	clarity, truth, breakthrough	emotional renewal, rebirth, creative spark
2 DUALITY	envision a plan, make a decision	need for balance, adaptability	indecision, stalemate, choices, dilemma	connection, unity, partnership, balance
3 GROWTH	explore, expand, embrace growth	collaboration, teamwork	heartache, sorrow, grief, loss	friendship, support, celebration
4 STABILITY	celebration, harmony and community	material possessions, security, stability	rest, relaxation, contemplation	apathy, introspection, doubt, stagnation
5 CHANGE	conflict, struggle, competition, defense	scarcity, hardship, poverty, struggle	conflict, tension, defeat, regret	loss, grief, regret, forgiveness
6 HARMONY	victory, recognition, success, leadership	generosity, charity, fairness, grace	transition, journey, progress	nostalgia, memory, childhood
7 FAITH	perseverance, faith, determination	patience, commitment	deception, cunning, strategy, stealth	illusion, choices, creative ideation
8 PROGRESS	rapid movement, action, swift progress	skill development, hard work, details	restriction, bondage, fear, paralysis	moving on, closure, abandonment
9 FRUITION	resilience, caution, defense of goals	self-sufficiency, luxury, independence	anxiety, worry, stress, despair	fulfillment, success, gratitude, abundance
10 COMPLETION	overwhelming burden or responsibility	legacy, wealth, family, heritage	endings, pain, release, renewal	bliss, harmony, ephemeral joy, beauty
PAGE EXPLORATION	passion, inspiration for a new project	new opportunities, desire for learning	curiosity, new mindset/beliefs	creativity, romance, sensitivity
KNIGHT MOTION	restless energy for action and adventure	hard work, dilligence, practical abundance	ambition, action, speed, courage,	charm, passion, idealism, pusuit
QUEEN MATURITY	confidence, charisma, inspiring to others	practical security, nurturing self	independence, boundaries, truth	empathy, intuition, kindness, nuture
KING AUTHORITY	leadership, vision, control, mastery	material success, responsibility	authority, wisdom, decisiveness	emotional maturity, compassion

Using Tarot Cards
preparation and spreads

The only required elements of a tarot reading are your deck and your focused intention. The quality of your question will dictate the quality of the response you recieve, so try to craft your questions with clarity, honesty and an attitude of detachment to the outcome.

1. To cleanse your deck's energy and imbue it with your own, you can pass it through incense or smudge it with herbs.

2. Choose a spread for your reading, appropriate to your intention/question (*example spreads are given below, opposite and throughout the book*).

3. Sit quietly with your deck, centre yourself and focus on the question.

4. Shuffle the deck, with an attitude of openness to what the tarot has to share with you. Focus on the overall purpose of the reading.

5. Draw a card for each question or position in the spread.

6. Consider each card's visual symbolism, meanings, and how it relates to its position in the spread.

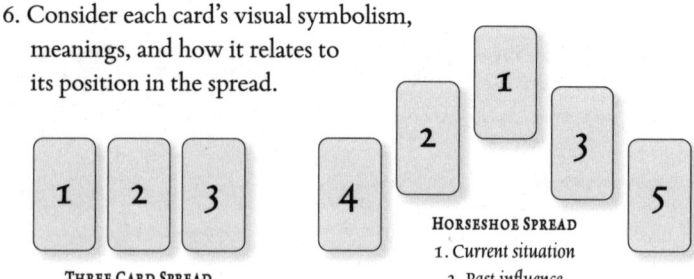

THREE CARD SPREAD
1. Desire 2. Obstacle 3. Solution

HORSESHOE SPREAD
1. Current situation
2. Past influence
3. Heart of the Matter 4. Obstacles 5. Outcome

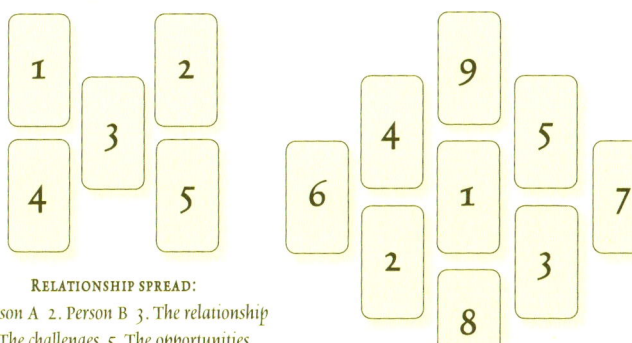

RELATIONSHIP SPREAD:
1. Person A 2. Person B 3. The relationship
4. The challenges 5. The opportunities

NINE CARD SPREAD: 1. The Situation 2. What to avoid 3. What to pursue 4. What is in the way 6. Past influences 7. Potential outcome 8. What is beneath you 9. The Crown, overall summary

NEW GROWTH SPREAD: 1. Self 2. Current situation 3. What to release 4. What to invite in 5. New potential growth 6. How to support this growth

CELTIC CROSS SPREAD (Trad.) 1. This is you 2. This crosses you 3. This crowns you 4. This is beneath you 5. This is behind you 6. This is before you 7. This is your attitude 8. These influence you 9. These are your hopes and fears 10. This is the outcome for you

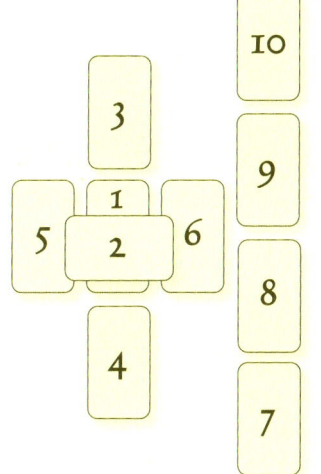

0 - ♅ THE FOOL △ - א
at the threshold

The FOOL is the first card in the Major Arcana, yet is numbered zero (*the fertile void*). He lacks experience but teems with unlimited potential, encountering and assimilating each archetypal lesson along the "Fool's Journey." He is dressed colourfully and travels light (*detachment from material existence*). He doesn't follow his feet (*reason, logic*), but looks to the sky (*universal principles*) while carrying a wand (*active will*) from which his baggage dangles behind him (*past experience*). A small dog (*intuitive nature*) spurs him onward even as he approaches a cliff edge, signalling his trust in fate and life. Some decks include a sun symbol, revealing his divine source of guidance.

Astrologically, the Fool corresponds to the planet Uranus (*unexpected change, liberation*) and the element of air (*intellect, innovation*). During the Medieval era, many royal courts employed a jester who used humour and satire to challenge authority. Laughter disarms reason and unlocks the gates of the conscious mind.

The Fool subverts expectations. Wise in innocence, he reminds us that wisdom can be found in unexpected places. When we access the pure, undifferentiated consciousness of the Fool (*the eternal Self*), we can transcend conventional ideas and processes that have long been stagnant.

ABOVE:

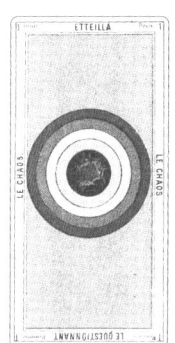

THE FOOL — a Leap of Faith: Unbound potential, the urge for freedom and expansion, breakthroughs, new ventures and insights, play and experimentation, innate abilities that allow one to overcome obstacles, innovation and originality, rewards for taking risks.
REVERSED: uncertainty about a new venture, self-doubt or indecision, the persistent feeling that one must learn more before doing, reckless extremes of behavior with a blind eye towards consequences, unaware of authentic desires, fear of taking risks.

1. INNER STATE 2. OUTER STATE

MIRROR SPREAD:
1. THE INNER STATE: THE FOOL – an inner awareness of freedom, limitless possibility, and a willingness to take risks. 2. THE OUTER STATE: – SEVEN OF WANDS – a defensive situation, operating from the belief that the position must be guarded. This suggests a need to reconcile the healthy desire to protect while maintaining the openness of The Fool.

1 - ☿ THE MAGICIAN ▵ - ב
between heaven and earth

The MAGICIAN begins the journey from creative possibility to material realization, transforming the unfocused promise of the Fool by directing his energy towards concrete ends. The lemniscate (∞) above his head represents infinite potential and connection to the eternal.

The Magician is associated with the planet Mercury and the Greek god Hermes, who travels between between celestial and earthly realms. Tilting one end of his wand (*will*) to the sky (*superconscious*) and the other to earth (*the material*), his gesture acts as a metaphor for the Hermetic axiom "*As Above, So Below*", a reminder that humanity is a microcosm of the universal macrocosm. Across his table (*the field of attention*) lie

tools representing the four suits of the Minor Arcana and the four elements of Nature: Wands (*Fire-Creativity*), Cups (*Water-Intuition*), Swords (*Air-Intellect*), and Pentacles (*Earth-Action*). The Magician's mastery of the elements enables him to give tangible form to ethereal inspiration, bringing ideas and dreams into concrete reality.

Despite the tools on the Magician's table, it is the creative, focused power of conscious intention that alchemically transforms base elements into something more valuable and refined, turning potential into being.

THE MAGICIAN — Manifestation of Willpower: Creative consciousness, ingenuity, intelligence, active focus, possessing creative or material resources, a swift mind, the ability to create reality in accordance with one's will, forging a singular path, ambition, mastery of a craft, the arts.

REVERSED: untapped or under-developed skills, feeling disempowered, weak-willed, distraction or procrastination, self-deception, illusion over substance, deception, misuse of power, overly self-focused.

ABOVE: The Magician, Bateleur "Juggler", from the 17th C. Tarot de Paris deck. FACING PAGE: From the Stefano Vergnano deck, Italy, 1826.

1. HIDDEN   2. KNOWN   3. REVEALED

CONCEALED & REVEALED SPREAD: **1. HIDDEN FROM CONSCIOUS AWARENESS:** FIVE OF WANDS — an internal struggle, where differing parts of self vie for expression. **2. WHAT IS KNOWN:** THE MAGICIAN — the conscious awareness that one possesses the tools to bring this creative tension to life, in material form. **3. NEW INFORMATION:** FIVE OF PENTACLES — draw on these inner resources and capacity for manifestation to endure challenging times ahead.

2 - ☽ THE HIGH PRIESTESS ▽ - ב
the inner mirror

The HIGH PRIESTESS (2) follows the Magician (1) and thus represents the emerging principle of duality within the tarot. She sits between two pillars (*polarity, conscious and subconscious*), wearing a crossed sash (*neutrality*) and holding a volume of esoteric wisdom. Behind, a pomegranate-print veil (*the underworld*) marks the threshold between two worlds (*profane and sacred*), signifiying the need to look beyond the surface to deeper truths. Unlike the Magician (*active, conscious manifestation*), she embodies the receptive, subconscious, feminine principle—understood through direct contact with the Mysteries (*gnosis*), requiring inner exploration, meditation and intuition.

Astrologically, she corresponds to the Moon (*emotions, memory*), shown as a crescent at the base of her flowing garments (*the primordial matrix*). Her element, water, is harmonised with the Moon's cycles of time, tide, and the rhythms of nature.

The subconscious mind, veiled from conscious awareness, is the record keeper of all events, and the High Priestess points to this hidden treasure trove (*her book or scroll*), reminding us that the inner mysteries hold the richest treasures. Illuminated by moonlight, the High Priestess accesses the deep wisdom and intuitive insights that arise from the mirror within.

THE HIGH PRIESTESS – the Mysteries of the Subconscious: Intuitive wisdom, spirituality, the subconscious, memory and dreamwork, inner exploration, clairvoyant or psychic abilities, mystical study and experience, receptivity, esoteric study, gnosis, hidden or unseen forces, meaning or answer unknown at this time.

REVERSED: Disconnection from intuition and spirituality, needing to go within, secrets, information withheld, error or duplicity, feeling misunderstood, withdrawn, alone or isolated; difficulty reaching out to others, a period of introspection, moodiness, need for solitude or emerging from a period of isolation.

LEFT: The High Priestess, La Papesse, from the Oswald Wirth Deck, 1889. FACING PAGE: Paris, 12th century. BELOW: In the Rider Waite deck, 1909, she sits between Boaz and Jachin, the entrance pillars to Solomon's Temple. She holds a scroll marked "TORA." Pomegranates (fertility and sacred wisdom) adorn the curtain behind.

1. HEART OF THE MATTER   2. CHALLENGE   3. PAST INFLUENCE   4. FORECAST

UNDER THE SURFACE SPREAD: 1. THE HEART OF THE MATTER: NINE OF SWORDS – stress & anxiety caused by worry & fear. 2. THE CHALLENGE: PAGE OF SWORDS – gaining control over negative thoughts by approaching them with energy, curiosity, and new perspectives. 3. ALL INFLUENCED BY: HIGH PRIESTESS – a previous period of inner exploration marked by solitude & isolation. 4. THE FORECAST: KING OF PENTACLES – participation in the material reality brings success & self-respect.

3 - ♀ THE EMPRESS ▽ - ♐
the transcendent third

Following the Magician (*singular, conscious creation*) and the High Priestess (*duality, subconscious reflection*), the EMPRESS embodies the fertile aspect of the feminine archetype—the ability to nurture life and to give birth to creative desires. She is at home in nature, sitting secure and relaxed amid buzzing pollinators and verdant growth. A crown of 12 stars (*zodiacal cycle*) connects her to the celestial realm and her scepter balances the power of human will (*below*) with the divine (*above*). The pomegranates on her dress allude to fecundity and rebirth. A shield (*protection*) bears a flying eagle (*freedom*).

Her number, 3, embodies creative synthesis and integration—from the union of one and two a third is born; a child, a work of art, a solution to a problem. Her element is Earth, and the symbol of Venus (*love, beauty*) is etched onto her throne, signalling her connection to harmony, abundance and relationships of all kinds.

The Empress exhibits creativity as an expression of love. Her ability to harness nature for creation and growth frees us from the limits of dualism to birth transcendent forms, relationships, and experiences of beauty.

FAR LEFT: Marseilles Tarot, 1760. CENTRE LEFT, Milan c.1810. RIGHT: The Etteilla Tarot, France, 1789.

THE EMPRESS – Nurturing Creativity and Abundance: The Mother, giving birth (to beings or projects), the forces of attraction, fertility, creative energy, abundance and prosperity, the healing power of nature, harmony and pleasure, grace and beauty, love and friendship, sensuality, aesthetic and artistic inspiration. REVERSED: Love or nurturing withheld, difficulty in receiving pleasure, creative blocks, self-indulgence, overly focused on material matters, needing to ground one's energy and refill one's own cup, a desire to reconnect to nature.

1. SITUATION   2. CONFLICT

CRUX SPREAD:
1. THE SITUATION: THE EMPRESS – one's desire to connect with one's creativity and the sensual pleasures of embodied living.
2. THE CONFLICT: TEN OF CUPS – an obligation to a family or group whom one belongs. The duties involved in this may be at odds with the desire to indulge in one's personal connection to their creative or artistic expression.

4 - ♈ THE EMPEROR △ - ה
inner authority

The abundance of the Empress (*creative synthesis*) finds stability in the EMPEROR. His number, 4, reflects order and balance—the four suits of the tarot, the four points of the compass, the four posts of the Magician's table. His element is fire and his shape, the square, is found wherever human order is imposed onto nature.

The bearded Emperor sits as a lone sentry, cross-legged on a cubed throne, with an empty sky and a wall of mountains (*challenges*) behind him. Wearing a heavy crown (*authority*), he grips his belt (*restriction*) for he renounced the freedom (*eagle*) of the Empress to serve as a guardian. He wears armor (*protection*) beneath his robes, yet carries no weapon, only a scepter or ankh (*life force*) to establish dominion. The rams carved into his throne point to Aries, the first sign of the zodiac, associated with the phrase *I am*—a declaration of singular will driving him on, reflecting the Emperor's empowered individuality and authority.

The Emperor builds the structures and discipline which allow goals to be achieved, but cautions against being too rigid or controlling. He protects his realm by establishing boundaries while respecting the sovereignty of others, revealing that true power comes from taking responsibility for one's choices.

THE EMPEROR – Authority and Structured Leadership: The archetypal father, stability, structure, control, personal responsibility, agency, authority figures, inner authority, autonomy, boundaries within relationships, protecting one's energy, habits and routines that allow us to thrive, the process of editing, refining, and pruning; taking a stand, assuming a position of leadership, the rational and logical mind. REVERSED: a need to be assertive, disconnection from inner power, rigidity, stubbornness, the desire for control, calcified structures or traditions, the need to break out of a routine or neglecting necessary routines, a corrupt leader, abuse of power.

1. STRENGTHS   2. WEAKNESSES

STRATEGY SPREAD:
1. **STRENGTHS:** THE PAGE OF PENTACLES – enterprising, trustworthy, and adaptable qualities; enthusiasm for a new project or venture that can bring material support.
2. **WEAKNESSES:** THE EMPEROR – suggests rigidity, stubbornness, or difficulty taking action due to an inability to claim a sense of authority or agency for oneself.

5 - ♉ THE HIEROPHANT ▽ - ו
sacred bridge

In Ancient Greece, the chief priest, or HIEROPHANT, interpreted the sacred Mysteries. A counterpart to the High Priestess, whose spiritual authority comes from within, the Hierophant acts as a bridge between the sacred and the mundane, transmitting the deeper meaning of arcane knowledge and bringing it down to Earth. He aligns with the zodiacal Taurus (*principles, stability*), an Earth sign that rules the throat, allowing him to give voice to the wisdom he perceives.

Two plus three equals five—the number of the Hierophant. He gives the sign of benediction to two students; two pairs of fingers representing the concealed (*esoteric*) and revealed (*exoteric*) doctrines. At his feet lay two crossed keys (*the keys to heaven*), showing that his insights are inaccessible without translation. Three appears in his triple crown and papal cross. Five itself correlates to æther—the fifth element, the *quintessence* of the alchemists—which links the human and the divine, encompassing and superseding the four elements of the natural world.

The Hierophant encourages moral discipline and adherence to tradition when it serves to liberate the spirit, but if the quest for enlightenment is distorted through dogma and hypocrisy, he can signal the need to break convention and forge a new path. As a conduit for higher wisdom, the Hierophant represents the humility to remain free of corruption, to be a channel for truth.

ABOVE: The Hierophant carries the papal cross and gives the gesture of benediction.

THE HIEROPHANT — *Spiritual Guidance and Tradition*: Interpreter of sacred mysteries, spiritual discipline, orthodoxy, an authority figure, working within institutions or large organizations, education, teaching, public speaking, counseling, the need for a trusted authority or mediator.
REVERSED: dogmatism, the distortion of truth, hypocrisy, deception or concealment, nonconformity, rebellion, iconoclasm, persecution for diverging from orthodoxy, distrust of religious authority, overly concerned with societal approval, a fallen guru.

1. FEARS 2. HOPES 3. REALITY

PERCEPTION-REALITY SPREAD: 1. FEARS: KING OF SWORDS — *fear of embodying a position of authority relying too heavily on logic and rationality to make decisions.* **2. HOPES:** THE HIEROPHANT — *hoping to hold a position of authority based on a connection to faith, values, or guiding spiritual principles.* **3. REALITY:** TWO OF PENTACLES — *the condition of using both logic and intuition to flow with the currents of life, and achieve an internal and external balance.*

6 - ♊ THE LOVERS △ - ♈
growth through relationship

The LOVERS depicts two people (*connection, relationship*) and as such, we enter the realm of individuated conscious choice. In the perfect Garden of Eden, primordial Woman stands to the left with the Tree of Knowledge (*temptation*), while on the right primordial Man stands with the Tree of Life (*redemption*). The man (*conscious*) looks to the woman (*subconscious*), who gazes up at an angel (*superconscious*). An absence of clothing reveals their fallibility and raw humanity.

In the zodiac, the Lovers corresponds to the air sign Gemini (*communication, reflection*), emphasizing that growth is experienced through relationships and dialogue. The angel, as a messenger of divine will, appears to be urging the two individuals to find wholeness by integrating the qualities of the other. The Lovers' number, 6, correlates to the hexagram ✡: the union of macrocosm (*above* △) and microcosm (*below* ▽).

The Lovers speak to significant turning points which are predicated on consequential choices and commitments. A wound (*arrow*) may accompany such a resolution, as selecting one path precludes others. Through cultivating discernment and making decisions from the higher self (*angel, inspiration*) comes the opportunity to evolve as individuals.

THE LOVERS – Choice and Union of Opposites: Growth through relationships, working in partnership, cooperation, choosing between paths, taking responsibility for one's choices, reckoning with concepts of free will vs. fate, love or lust, a passionate union, balancing head with heart.
REVERSED: a feeling of separation or alienation, self-reliance, jealousy or possessiveness, feeling torn between two choices or paths, uncertainty around a relationship, head and heart not aligned.

BELOW: Rider Waite deck: The gaze flows from Adam to Eve to the angel, forming an upward triangle.

HOLD & RELEASE SPREAD:
1. EMBRACE: THE LOVERS— suggests embracing a meaningful relationship based on an alignment of values & mutual respect. Honest communication, vulnerability & openness are important for a harmonious and deep bond.
2. LET GO OF: FIVE OF SWORDS— suggests letting go of resentments about past conflicts where heated words were exchanged, or times when one felt rejected by another.

1. EMBRACE

2. RELEASE

7 - ♋ THE CHARIOT ▽ - ♊
overcoming obstacles

The CHARIOT is the culmination of the previous cards, and includes symbolism from them. Wearing a victor's laurel wreath beneath a crown (*the Empress*), a charioteer stands under a celestial canopy (*divine guidance*). A pair of horses (*progress*) or sphinxes (*mystery*) pull the chariot, the dual forces balanced (*the Lovers*). He wears armour under vestments adorned with zodiacal imagery, crescent moons (*the High Priestess*) encircling his shoulders. He leaves a city (*the Emperor's domain*) on a journey into the unknown (*the Fool*), his chariot guided (*the Hierophant*) with a wand (*the Magician*), affirming the control he has over the power of his will.

Astrologically he corresponds to the water sign Cancer (*the crab; emotional, nuturing*), whose protective shell can be likened to the charioteer's vehicle. The chariot's number 7 is connected to complete systems—the seven acts of creation in Genesis, the seven stages of transformation in alchemy, the seven visible planets, the seven days of the week, the seven chakras.

The card emphasizes the carriage over the driver, suggesting that if the personality evolves without inflation or hubris, it can become a vehicle for higher forces to manifest the deeper self.

THE CHARIOT – Triumphant Willpower and Determination: Overcoming obstacles, moving purposefully towards a goal, worldly ambition, willpower, a desire for visibility and success, emotional self-control, rapid momentum, tenacity, hard shell but soft interior. REVERSED: ego-directed goals that don't align with the higher self, reticence to pursuing goals, fear of failure, stagnation, reconsidering direction, blockage of energy, outgrowing an old sense of self.

1. KNOWN

2. UNKNOWN

NEW DIRECTION SPREAD:
1. **WHAT IS KNOWN:** EIGHT OF CUPS – leave a situation or relationship which is no longer emotionally fulfilling. 2. **WHAT IS UNKNOWN:** THE CHARIOT – where will this decision lead to? Does one have the will to to leave? 3. **THE CHALLENGE:** THREE OF CUPS – find new relationships which nurture the desire for authentic connection built on collaboration. 4. **THE OPPORTUNITY:** KING OF CUPS – approach new connections from a place of emotional maturity. 5. **THE OUTCOME:** THREE OF WANDS – these new relations expand one's horizons, and bring one out into the world in a new way.

3. CHALLENGE

4. OPPORTUNITY

5. OUTCOME

8 - ♌ STRENGTH △ - ♃
light and shadow

While the Chariot represents an individual's mastery over the environment, STRENGTH illustrates inner mastery through emotional courage. A woman in a white gown (*purity*) patiently tames a lion (*passion, base instincts*), not by force but by the establishment of mutual trust. Her magic is accomplished gently through her presence alone, without wand or contrivance. Like the Magician (*active concentration*), the lemniscate (∞) vibrates over her head, signifying the harmonization of opposites within the psyche which allows her to attain self-awareness.

Strength's number, 8, symbolizes balance and stability. She connects to the fire sign of Leo (*confidence, charisma*). The zodiac's lion is associated with the Sun and thus the heart—the organ of love and seat of the will. Alchemically, the heart transmutes fear into fortitude.

The lion represents the raw, primal force of the unconscious or irrational emotions that have the potential to consume us (*the shadow*). Yet as Strength suggests, by befriending the inner wild animal with compassion and an open heart, we may more purposefully shape our lives, allowing the authentic self to emerge.

STRENGTH—Inner Courage and Gentle Mastery: The triumph of love over fear, compassionate strength, recognizing and accepting instinctual nature, the application of gentle force, self-knowledge and self-acceptance, inner wisdom, overcoming conflict by bringing in a higher energy.
REVERSED: excessive use of force, fighting fire with fire, fear of true emotions or desires, stubbornness, holding back, masking tenderness with bravado, difficulty being vulnerable with others, indifference, a need to reinforce emotional boundaries.

ABOVE: LEFT: Tarot Belgijski, 1780. The lemniscate forms the hat. RIGHT: Mantegna Tarot, c.1465. FACING PAGE: The Etteilla Tarot, France, 1789.

1. GOAL

2. OBSTACLE

3. HELP

BREAKTHROUGH SPREAD: 1. THE GOAL: STRENGTH—remain calm and focused, and draw on one's courage to face an obstacle or challenge, either internally (as a persistent fear) or externally (as another situation). 2. THE OBSTACLE: KNIGHT OF SWORDS—speaking/behaving in a brash and impulsive manner, or rushing to a conclusion. 3. THE HELP: ACE OF SWORDS—create a quiet, calm environment to meditate and then respond with clarity rather than reacting to the challenge at hand.

9 - ♍ THE HERMIT ▽ - ,
inward search

Cloaked in a gray robe (*emotional detachment*), the HERMIT appears as a wise elder holding a lantern (*illumination*), journeying alone with his staff through dark silent regions to bring forth inner light. Like the Fool, he is a wanderer and a seeker. In early decks the Hermit was shown as Father Time with an hourglass, signalling that wisdom is accumulated with patience and experience.

The bearded Hermit is a mystic, forging his own path to revelation in solitude. Removed from worldly concerns, his guidance comes from within. He is connected with the zodiacal Earth sign Virgo (*detailed, analytical*), exemplifying striving, refinement and the dedication necessary for personal development.

His number, 9, represents completion and initiation, the end of one of one cycle before the birth of a new manifestation—human life gestates in nine months, initiation into the Eleusinian mysteries took nine days, Roman dead were buried on the ninth day, Apollonius of Tyana kept the ninth hour for silence.

The title of this card suggests the *hermetic seal*—the isolation necessary to nurture the inner flame and contact the deepest self. The Hermit advises shielding our lantern (*the light of consciousness*) with the cloak of solitude, to protect it from the elements (*the expectations and demands of others*).

LEFT: The Hermit is shown with an hourglass, as Father Time and later with a lantern. Cards from the Visconti Sforza deck, Milan, c.1450; Ancient Tarot of Lombardy, Milan, 1810; The Etteilla Tarot, France, 1789.

THE HERMIT – Wisdom through Solitude and Reflection: A seeker of knowledge, spiritual growth, self-reflection and silence, turning attention inward, withdrawal from society for a period of time, following inner guidance, a strong inner compass, guidance and mentorship, seeking deeper meaning and purpose. REVERSED: fear of carving one's own path, discomfort with solitude, distractions from inner work, inability to quiet the mind, enforced solitude, seeking spirit in unholy places or people, returning to the world after a period of introversion.

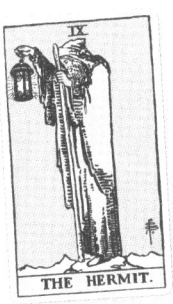   

1. MENTAL   2. PHYSICAL   3. EMOTIONAL   4. SPIRITUAL

FOUR ELEMENTS SPREAD: 1. MENTALLY: THE HERMIT – contemplative and drawn towards activities and practices which support self-reflection, solitude and study. 2. PHYSICALLY: SIX OF WANDS – energized and in command of one's physical body. 3. EMOTIONALLY: THREE OF PENTACLES – hopeful and well-resourced. 4. SPIRITUALLY: THE HANGED MAN – learning the deepest lessons through the art of surrender.

10 – 4 WHEEL OF FORTUNE △ - כ
change as constant

Following the Hermit's inner illumination, the ever-turning WHEEL OF FORTUNE compels the acceptance of forces outside our control. A mighty wheel reigns over the mechanism of fate (*karma*). A dog (*Anubis*; *afterlife*) ascends the wheel (*good fortune*), while a snake (*Typhon*; *chaos*) slithers down. In the corners, four creatures (*bull*, *eagle*, *lion*, *angel*) hint at other fours—the Evangelists, the fixed signs of the zodiac, the elements of Nature, the suits of Tarot. The sphinx (*riddles*, *destiny*), a synthesis of the four creatures, sits atop the wheel (*equilibrium*) holding a sword (*truth*), representing higher, cosmic law.

Aligned with the planet Jupiter (*expansion*, *luck*), the Wheel is the pivotal midpoint of the journey. Its number ten appears as a Roman numeral 'X' in the stable center, representing a return to unity (1) and the start of a new cycle (0).

Even as the Wheel creates the flux of life's ups and downs, the still, stationary elements (*the center*, *the Sphinx*, *the four creatures*) are a reminder of the responsibilties and control we have over intentions or choices. Cultivating detachment from its constant motion allows us to remain steady in the face of difficulties, centered in the knowledge that the Wheel will turn again.

LEFT: Early Fortune cards, c.1715, 1810, 1789. BELOW: In the Rider-Waite version, the wheel is engraved with "ROTA" (Latin-wheel), four alchemical symbols, and the Hebrew name of God in the YHVH tetragram.

THE WHEEL OF FORTUNE – Cycles of Change and Destiny: Change as the eternal constant, seizing a moment of opportunity, being at the right place at the right time, an unexpected change of fortune, overcoming setbacks, a turning point, force majeure, going with the flow, taking responsibility for the past. REVERSED: repeating past patterns, resistance to change, trying to swim upstream, needing greater willpower, not taking responsibility for previous actions, circular thinking.

1. CAUSES   2. CURRENT SITUATION   3. OUTCOME

ORIGIN & DESTINY SPREAD: 1. THE CAUSE: TEN OF PENTACLES – desire for a long-term partnership that can support a family or legacy. 2. THE SITUATION: TWO OF PENTACLES – the rebalancing of resources to achieve stability. 3. THE OUTCOME: WHEEL OF FORTUNE – a significant, positive turning point, marked by fated events outside one's control.

11 - ♎ JUSTICE △ - ל
truth and consequences

Whereas the Wheel of Fortune represents the principle of cosmic balance outside the individual's control, JUSTICE explores the concept of balance within an individual's control. As such, it is concerned with fairness, principled action, and ethics. A crowned and robed woman sits enthroned (*authority*) between two pillars (*stability, balance*) holding scales (*equilibrium, neutrality*) that move perpetually as she weighs and measures all factors with impartiality. Her sword (*reason, precision*) points toward the heavens, for her judgement is in alignment with the higher principles of Truth.

Justice connects with the air sign Libra in the zodiac (*the scales; equality, balance*) and her number is 11, a visual symbol of symmetry and equilibrium.

The ideals of Justice are not a neat system of punishment and reward; her concern is with the maintenance of universal harmony, without bias or prejudice. The scales signify the creative and dynamic perpetual rebalancing of opposing forces, while her sword cuts through illusions and excuses, enabling us to act in accordance with our principles, taking full responsibility for the consequences of all our actions.

JUSTICE – Fair and Balanced Judgment: the pursuit of fairness, balance, and harmony, compensation for losses, a need to dispassionately weigh the pros and cons to arrive at a conclusion, acting out of a concern for fairness to the self, getting one's dues, cutting through illusions and fantasies. REVERSED: emotions overpowering intellect, inner disharmony, overly focused on unfair situations outside of one's control, making peace with unfairness, prejudice or bias, situations involving the law or the courts, an unfair situation, unable to see clearly.

Justice cards. ABOVE: LEFT: Italy, 1465. RIGHT: Milan, c.1450. FACING PAGE: France, 1789.

1. MESSAGE

2. CHALLENGE

3. ADVICE

ADVICE SPREAD: 1. THE MESSAGE: SIX OF PENTACLES—*cultivate a generous and charitable spirit towards others, and to give what one can financially, emotionally, or in terms of one's time.* **2. THE CHALLENGE:** FOUR OF PENTACLES—*it is difficult to give freely when one clinging to what one has, or if one has adopted a mindset of scarcity.* **3. THE ADVICE:** JUSTICE—*one must act in accordance with one's higher moral principles, and not from a place of fear.*

12 - ♆ THE HANGED MAN ▽ - מ
surrender

After the reckoning of Justice, we turn towards acceptance and surrender in the HANGED MAN. Suspended between two trees (*heaven and earth, material and spiritual*), the Hanged man dangles from one leg, the other bent behind (*the cross*). With his heart placed above his head (*intellect*), he submits his personal will to the divine (*superconscious*), serenely sacrificing his individual desires in service of a larger process.

The Hanged Man is associated with watery Neptune (*illusions, spirituality, the dissolution of ego*). His number, 12, links to many cosmic and earthly cycles: 12 signs of the zodiac, 12 months of the year, 12 hours of the day. His number and posture are inversions of the final Major Arcana card, the World (21), revealing the necessity of releasing attachments and surrendering the ego on the journey towards true freedom and fulfillment.

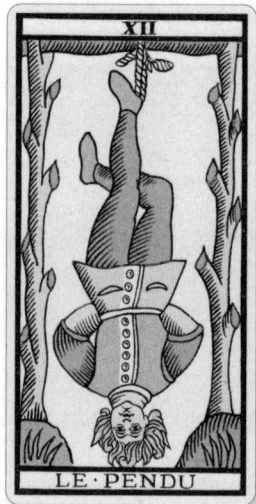

The Tree of Life (*p.vi*) is a central symbol in Judaic Kabbalah, while in Norse mythology, the god Odin hung himself on the world tree Yggdrasil for nine days to gain spiritual wisdom. Results can take time and patience to manifest, yet, like Odin, the Hanged Man's reversal can facilitate shifts in perspective to give fresh insights. This liminal state can be likened to an initiation rite, where the old self is sacrificed so that the new can emerge.

LEFT: Early versions show the Hanged Man holding two bags. In later versions his hands are hidden behind his back. FAR LEFT: Charles VI Tarot.

THE HANGED MAN – Surrender and New Perspective: Sacrifice, releasing an old version of self, a shift in perspective, a reversal of circumstance, spiritual growth through turning inward, a period of inactivity, enduring stagnancy with grace, forgiveness of self and others, a period of gestation, feeling suspended between old and new. REVERSED: discomfort with stagnancy, fighting against the flow of life, clinging to old ways, inability to surrender, forcing activity when rest is needed, neglecting the spiritual dimension of life, confusion, depression, feeling persecuted by others, a need to forgive oneself or others.

1. PAY ATTENTION TO   2. SUGGESTED ACTION

BLIND SPOT SPREAD:
1. PAY ATTENTION TO: KNIGHT OF CUPS – suggests a desire to channel imagination into a gift, work of art, or creative project inspired by a depth of feeling and reverence for beauty. 2. SUGGESTED ACTION: THE HANGED MAN – counsels one to suspend daily habits and routines in order to access deeper states of consciousness.

13 - ♏ DEATH ▽ - ♪
sunset, sunrise

If the Hanged Man symbolizes a leaf's fall, DEATH signifies the active process of its decay and rebirth as part of the soil. Death, personified as a skeleton, wields a scythe. In the Rider-Waite-Smith deck, it wears black (*loss*) armour and carries a flag bearing a white rose (*renewal*). It rides a pale horse, trampling those before it, yet hope appears in the distance, the sun rising in the east (*rebirth*) between two pillars (*liminality*).

Though Death comes for all—peasants, bishops, and kings alike—its appearance in the middle of the Major Arcana reveals that it does not represent the end but rather a significant stage of change and transformation along the Fool's Journey.

Death is associated with the water sign of Scorpio (*the scorpion*; *resilience, regeneration*) and the number 13. Although linked to superstition and bad luck, many flowering plants use 5, 8 and 13 in their growth patterns, while in Egyptian mythology the dismembered body of Osiris is remade by Isis from 13 pieces.

The body of flesh and bones returns to Earth, yet is not our true nature. The more we can identify with the inner self, the greater our capacity to live meaningfully. Death contains a paradox: it is not the opposite of life—birth is, while life encompasses it all.

DEATH — Profound Transformation and Change: Release, metamorphoses, harbinger of a new phase of life, the painful process of change, letting go, moving on, shattering or splintering the sense of self, major transition, clarity from new realizations, a rebirth process. REVERSED: resistant or fearful of change, feeling stuck or disappointed, inability to move on or let go, feeling blocked in a period of transition, resistance as the source of pain.

ABOVE: Death rakes the remnants of the field.

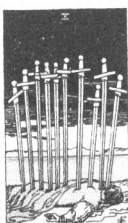

2. ROOT OF IT

3. PAST INFLUENCES

1. CURRENT STATE

4. ASPIRATIONS

5. GUIDANCE

CRUX SPREAD:
1. CURRENT STATE: EIGHT OF PENTACLES — hard work learning a new skill, which will lead to mastery. 2. ROOT OF THE SITUATION: TEN OF SWORDS — sudden end from a previous project or job which had run its course. 3. PAST INFLUENCES: SEVEN OF CUPS — disillusionment or confusion about one's options, and which path to take. 4. ASPIRATIONS: FOUR OF CUPS — carefully wait for the right opportunity to come along. 5. THE GUIDANCE: DEATH — fully release and grieve the passing of one life phase so that a new one can begin.

14 - ♐ TEMPERANCE △ - ♂
balance and integration

After loss through Death, TEMPERANCE appears as a healing balm, restoring internal balance. A winged angel (*divine messenger*) stands with one foot on water (*inner world, emotion*) and one on land (*outer world, form*). She pours water from one vessel to another below (*memories*) tempering her inner experience, like the tradition of mixing wine with water to dilute its potency. An orange triangle on her robe indicates the process of alchemy (*transmutation, purification*), integrating contrasting principles (*material and spiritual, masculine and feminine, conscious and unconscious*) into a unified whole.

Temperance corresponds to the fire sign Sagittarius, (*the archer; the quest for wisdom*). Her number, 14, marks a second cycle of seven in the Major Arcana, culminating the inward search for truth within the opposing forces of macrocosm and microcosm. The angel (*elevated self*) embodies the flow of current between the two vessels.

Temperance moves beyond dualistic thinking by embracing paradox and a multi-faceted reality. The integration of opposites, rather than negating either pole, supports peace, acceptance, and a sense of greater universal forces re-establishing inner harmony.

ABOVE: The angel stands on two different stones, as another depiction of opposing forces. Etteilla Tarot, 1789.

TEMPERANCE – Finding Balance and Harmony: Healing, resting, integrating opposite forces, restoring balance, tempering extremes of attitude or emotion, cooperation, balancing many tiers of awareness in the mind, inspiration, a rebirth after loss.
REVERSED: excess, extremes of emotion or behavior, volatility, mind or body out of balance, a need to focus on healing, a need to balance emotions.

1. SELF   2. OTHER

BOUNDARIES SPREAD:
1. **Self**: ACE OF PENTACLES— a focus on resources, with the drive to create oportunites to suport one's material existence.
2. **Other**: TEMPERANCE— this represents more of an internal focus, where healing and coming into alignment with the deep self takes priority over material matters.

15 - ♑ THE DEVIL ▽ - ע
facing inner monsters

A deficit of Temperance leads to expulsion from Eden. The Lovers now appear naked as hostages of the DEVIL, a winged demon with human and animal parts (*inner fragmentation*). They have horns and tails (*animalistic impulses*) revealing subservience to the lower aspects of self. The Devil acts as a totem for the fears, repressed instincts, and shame which keeps the chained pair unconsciously trapped in this situation.

The Devil's hand is branded with the symbol of Saturn, ruler of the Earth sign Capricorn (*the goat; ambition*). As Saturn is the planet of boundaries and restrictions, this card speaks to both being hampered by limitations, as well as overcoming them.

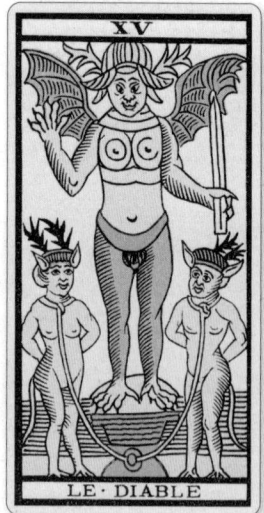

The Devil's number, 15, reduces to 6 (1 + 5, *the Lovers*; *choice*) reflecting the fallen couple's shadow side of greed and temptation. Their incarceration is an illusion, for they can choose to remove the chains (*limitations, unconscious agreements*) once they acknowledge their own sovereignty and exert their free will.

The Devil personifies the excesses, intoxications, and ideologies for which humans give up their freedom. Feelings of entrapment or victimization can be dispelled by examining negative beliefs and misguided obsessions under the light of conscious awareness.

ABOVE: The left hand is raised while the right faces the ground, the opposite of the hand position of The Magician. Etteilla, 1789; Piedmontese Tarot, 1865.

THE DEVIL — Materialism, Temptation, and Bondage: Self-sabotage, shame, addiction, confronting inner fears and limiting beliefs, conditions which prevent growth, overly focused on material matters, false idols, a need to overcome negative influences, contacting true inner desires, creative breakthroughs. REVERSED: breaking free of bondage or toxic habits, leaving an unhealthy relationship, detachment from unhealthy forces or thought patterns, decisions which empower, refusing to deal with a challenging situation, avoidance of truth, denial.

1. RELATIONSHIP   2. CHALLENGE   3. ADVICE

RELATIONSHIP ADVICE SPREAD: 1. THE RELATIONSHIP: NINE OF WANDS — one or both parties are behaving defensively, acting out of fear, or are overly guarded. 2. THE CHALLENGE: THE DEVIL — confront fears head-on, especially as they relate to fears of abandonment or conversely, codependence. 3. THE ADVICE: KNIGHT OF PENTACLES — patiently and steadily work towards a feeling of stability within the relationship, built on mutual trust and accountability.

16 - ♂ THE TOWER △ - פ
high brought low

While the Devil represents the prison of limiting beliefs, the TOWER depicts its sudden collapse, precipitating new revelations. A lightning bolt (*sudden insight*) strikes the Tower (*the defenses of the ego*), knocking off its crown (*glorified ideals*). Two figures (*the Lovers or builders*) tumble towards the ground (*humility*). The Tower suggests that if ambition is left unchecked, a sudden, unpredictable strike (*divine intervention*) will correct any disharmony by exposing its unstable foundation.

The Tower is astrologically linked with Mars (*desire, drive*), the firey spark that motivates action, for either constructive or destructive purposes. Its number 16 reduces to 7 (*the Chariot*) revealing the shadow side of determination and willpower—arrogance and hubris.

The Tarot originated in medieval Italy where towers reflected power and wealth, and as such the Tower symbolizes attempts to guard against the inevitable fluctuations of fate and circumstance. Unexpected change crumbles calcified beliefs and, while painful, may liberate us from unsustainable situations. The shock of disruption catalyzes the disintegration of stagnant patterns, bringing clarity and an opportunity to rebuild in harmony with higher principles.

THE TOWER — Sudden Upheaval and Revelation: Abrupt change or shift in perspective, revelations resulting from shocking events, profound realizations or a greater truth, epiphanies, a need to rebuild foundations, over-reaching or selfish ambition, lessons in humility, destroying the old to rebuild anew. REVERSED: revelations on an internal level, untenable situations which can no longer be endured, seeing through illusions or false impressions, rebuilding following collapse.

1. SITUATION   2. CHALLENGE   3. ADVICE

GENERAL ADVICE SPREAD: 1. THE SITUATION: NINE OF CUPS – one has attained a level of contentment and satisfaction in life, but it may be short lived due to a lack of spiritual development. 2. THE CHALLENGE: THE TOWER – an event or realization exposes the fragility of one's foundations, stripping away what provided a false sense of security. 3. THE ADVICE: SEVEN OF PENTACLES – patiently invest energy in what can produce sustainable long-term happiness.

17 - ♒ THE STAR △ - ♒

celestial waters

After the destruction of the Tower (*social persona, material attachments*) the naked (*pure*) STAR represents hope and renewal. Kneeling at a pond's edge (*subconscious, intuition*), she meditatively pours one vessel of water into the pool (*emotion*) and another onto land (*embodiment*). In contrast to Temperance (*balance*), the Star pours water in only one direction, symbolising energy flowing from conscious to unconscious.

The Star's number, 17, reduces to 8 (1+7), and in the sky above her blaze eight stars—radiant centers of light that link to deep time and connect to the cosmos. Each star has eight points, (*the compass, the North star*), pointing to an inner guiding principle that remains in times of uncertainty. Some decks show seven small stars (*the planets, the chakras, the Pleiades*) surrounding a larger one.

The Star aligns with the air sign Aquarius, the water-bearer of the zodiac, (*idealism, unity*). It signals a feeling of renewed hope and inspiration following a period of loss or challenge, and a focus on healing and replenishing the spirit. The Star reminds us that the spiral of evolution occurs through a process of remembering that our true nature is mirrored in the cosmic archetypes of the firmament above.

ABOVE: LEFT: An angel contemplates the stars, Tarot de Mantegna. c.1465. RIGHT: A woman combines the two waters, Etteilla Tarot, 1789.

THE STAR — Hope, Inspiration and Guidance: Emotional cleansing, renewal, a focus on healing, feeling connected to a larger meaningful pattern, engaging in ritual and ceremony, a period of reflection and contemplation, reconnecting with nature, regaining strength, new opportunities that bring hope. REVERSED: a need to focus on restoring health, feeling depleted emotionally or physically, a need for solitude, feeling isolated in struggles, dealing with illness, disconnection from nature, a lack of hope or optimism, a need to focus on what nourishes the spirit, a need for emotional release.

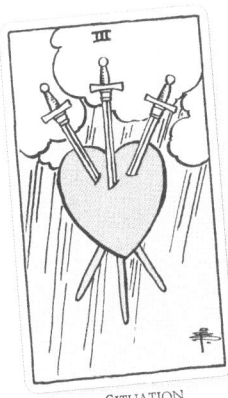
1. SITUATION

2. FEELING

3. SUGGESTED ACTION

FEELING & REACTION SPREAD: 1. SITUATION: THREE OF SWORDS – being broken-hearted, emotionally fragile or vulnerable, the importance of tending to these wounds. 2. FEELING: QUEEN OF CUPS – it is an opportunity to grow emotionally, and that by exploring the depths, one can emerge with treasures of wisdom. 3. SUGGESTED ACTION: THE STAR – embrace the process of renewal and spend time nurturing body, mind and spirit.

18 - ♓ THE MOON ▽ - ק
under Luna's reflection

After the conscious optimism of the Star, the MOON turns our focus inward. A crayfish (*primal self*) surfaces from a pool (*unconscious*) while a dog and wolf (*rational and intuitive instincts*) howl under the pale glow of the Moon. Two pillars on the horizon (*threshold of conscious mind*) separate the animal kingdom from the unseen realms beyond. Golden stars form the backdrop of the night sky, but the Moon, as the Earth's closest companion, pulls on the collective imagination and influences the rhythms of nature and the tides of life.

The Moon aligns with the water sign Pisces (*imagination, empathy, intuition*), and its number, 18, evokes the Hermit (1+8 = 9, *illumination in darkness*).

At night, Lunar consciousness reveals underlying feelings through dreams. As the Moon doesn't generate its own light, but reflects that of the Sun, it represents not the perceptions of waking consciousness, but rather what is revealed in the shadows. While in the clutches of the Moon's currents, fears and illusions may percolate, bringing awareness to lurking desires and concerns.

The Moon invites us to encounter the guardians at the gate of the subconscious, integrating the wisdom of the psyche's instinctual and primordial aspects.

LEFT: Michiate Deck, Florence c.1550; Tarocchini Luna, Bologna, c. 1490; Visconti Sforza deck c.1450. The Moon is often depicted as conjunct with the sun as an eclipse (e.g. in Rider-Waite deck, below).

THE MOON – Illusion, Intuition, and the Subconscious: Examining one's shadow or repressed desires, a focus on inner work, connecting to dreams, deep intuition, instinctual urges, changeability, moodiness, seeking comfort and protection, secrets or information withheld, psychic development, revelation of inner self. REVERSED: desires not consciously understood, an internal voyage, tension from resistance, feeling vulnerable or exposed, feelings of confusion or uncertainty finally subside.

1. PAST   2. PRESENT   3. FUTURE

TIME SPREAD: 1. PAST: TEN OF WANDS – an undertaking or major project completed with much laboring and effort. 2. PRESENT: THE MOON – This chapter has ended and one finds oneself in foggy terrain, unable to see the path ahead clearly. 3. FUTURE: PAGE OF CUPS – listen to intuitive hunches, dreams, and gut feelings, to feel towards surprising creative revelations.

19 - ☉ THE SUN △ - ר
divinity within

Following the subconscious reflection of the Moon, all is now seen clearly in the bright light of the SUN. A naked child (or children) (*innocence, purity*) plays inside a walled garden (*safety*) illuminated by the brilliant solar rays (*energy, success*). Reveling in freedom and spontaneity, they may be seen riding a white horse (*strength*). A crown (*enlightenment*) and banner (*celebration*) celebrate the embodiment of the authentic self, and the harmonious integration of instinct and ego. To be childlike—pure, open-hearted, and always in a stage of unfoldment—represents the path of self-actualization of the Sun.

Astrologically, the Sun—the center of the solar system—represents the essential, higher self and the creative realization of the will. The card's number, 19, reduces to ten (1 + 9 = 10, *Wheel of Fortune; change, destiny*) and thence to one (1 + 0 = 1, *the Magician; active manifestation*).

The Sun is worshiped in many cultures as a symbol of the godhead. Both are synonymous with sustaining life on Earth by emitting a radiance that cannot be looked at directly but rather perceived through the light of an inner divinity.

The Sun represents unity with the divine will and is a reminder of the joy, confidence, success and enlightenment which is our birthright when we align with our true nature.

ABOVE: Le Tarot Flamand, 1780; Rennaissance Tarot, c.1520 *The horse often has a solar correspondence.*

THE SUN *Joy, Clarity, and Success:* The conscious ego, creative willpower and self expression, health and vitality, accomplishment and success, clarity, liberation from struggle, confidence and talent, freedom and self-reliance, connection to the inner child, the divinity within. REVERSED: latent but untapped potential, difficulty accessing creativity, delayed success, feeling withdrawn, a desire for renewed energy in a project or relationship, the need to re-connect to the inner child, the potential for self-centeredness or hubris.

1. SELF   2. ONE'S PATH   3. ONE'S POTENTIAL

AUTHENTIC PATH SPREAD: 1. THE SELF: THE SUN — *one feels self-assured, confident, connected to authentic self expression, and creatively empowered.* 2. ONE'S PATH: QUEEN OF PENTACLES — *use the light of the Self to create financial abundance which can be used to help support and care for others.* 3. ONE'S POTENTIAL: FOUR OF WANDS — *celebrate these gains by sharing the bounty with others, and by taking pleasure in the company of friends.*

20 - ק JUDGEMENT △ - ש
reckoning and rebirth

With the spiritual awaking bestowed by the Sun comes responsibility and assesment. The JUDGEMENT card depicts direct communication between humanity and the divine. An angel (*the divine*) sounds its trumpet (*awakening*) over figures rising from their tombs (*resurrection*), hands raised to heaven (*integrating a higher calling*).

Judgement is associated with Pluto (*the underworld*), known to initiate intense psychic transformation prompted by forces beyond the individual's control. Its element is fire, and its number 20 reduces to 2, reflecting the High Priestess (*subconscious, dreams, memory*).

The themes of resurrection, self-evaluation, healing and absolution resurface in Ancient Greece, where Asclepius, the god of medicine, was purported to bring the dead back to life. Healing temples dedicated to him (*Asclepieia*), facilitated a focused, healing sleep for the sick, during which cures could be revealed through dreams.

Judgement calls for a personal rebirth by reckoning with past actions and by resolving to forgive and release the past. It can signify an awakened conscience with resolutions to live in alignment with higher values, as well as the opportunity to give birth to a new version of self.

JUDGEMENT – Rebirth and Self-assessment: a breakthrough, a spiritual awakening or call to awaken to a new level of consciousness, the need to evolve and grow, an important life lesson, events that catalyze personal growth, making decisions in alignment with one's best interests. REVERSED: avoidance of taking action, fear of making important changes or decisions, refusing to listen, a need to make amends (to self or others), a need to review the past in order to move forward, overly focused on judgement of others or self.

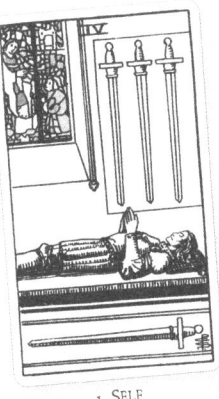

1. SELF 2. RELATIONSHIP 3. PARTNER

RELATIONSHIP SPREAD: 1. THE SELF: FOUR OF SWORDS – one feels withdrawn, contemplative, and in need of deep rest or recuperation. 2. THE RELATIONSHIP: EIGHT OF SWORDS – feels binding, stagnant or limiting, though in reality it may be the Self holding back. 3. THE PARTNER: JUDGEMENT – a rousing force who encourages one to integrate the lessons learned from the period of healing rest and to embrace the possibilities of a rebirth.

21 - ♄ THE WORLD ▽ - ת
task accomplished

Following the rebirth of Judgement, the WORLD brings culmination and fulfillment, completing the Great Work of the Major Arcana. A joyful dancing woman (*anima mundi–soul of the world*) is encircled by a laurel wreath (*victory*) wrapped in red bows that echo the lemniscates (*∞ infinite potential*) of the Magician (1) and Strength (8). The oval wreath (*the mandorla–heaven on Earth*) contains her energy so that she can move with the dynamic currents of the present. In each hand she holds a wand, symbolizing an ability to balance and integrate the many dualities of her journey. The wreath is flanked by four creatures—a man, an eagle, a lion and a bull (*the Evangelists, the fixed signs of the zodiac, the elements, the suits of the Minor Arcana, the four directions*).

The World's number, 21, combines 2 (*balance*) with 1 (*beginnings*), summing to 3 (*the Empress; creativity*). Astrologically, it corresponds to Saturn (*time, diligence*) whose limitations and structure create both new life and the senescence to which all eventually succumb.

The World moves perpetually between polarities, eternally dancing through ebbs and flows. The end may be a beginning, for her enclosing garland is also a portal, birthing the Fool (0) for a new cycle around Fortune's Wheel.

THE WORLD Fulfillment and Completion: Culmination, the attainment of a major undertaking, oneness with a greater calling, the ability to dialectically hold two opposing feelings, ideas or beliefs, the ability to synthesize opposing forces, a reciprocal or an ending which carries the seed of a new beginning.

1. SELF: 6S – in transitional phase, something left behind, destination unclear.

2. SITUATION: 2W – Taking initiative to seek broader horizons.

3. INFLUENCES: 7S – One cannot meet one's needs in the current situation.

4. SUBCONSCIOUS INFLUENCES: KW – Aspirations of power.

5. ROOT / PAST: AC – An emotional encounter or offer compelled one to action.

6. FUTURE INFLUENCES: 4C – Pausing to reflect and decide on incoming offers.

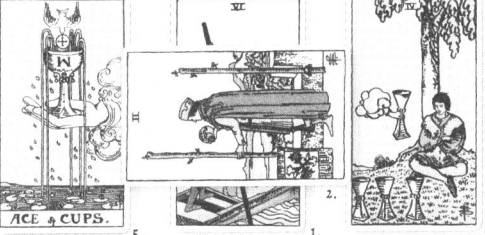

7. POWER IN SITUATION: QS – Using discrimination and logic to make choices aligned with one's highest good.

8. ENVIRONMENTAL INFLUENCES: QW – A successful mentor or mature role model is available to guide the way.

9. HOPES/FEARS: KnW – The hope for creative adventure. The fear of action or taking initiative.

10. OUTCOME: THE WORLD Accomplishment and success. Integration of lessons learned. A new start.

REVERSED: delayed culmination, an incomplete goal or undertaking, the ability to exist in a liminal condition, feeling daunted by a large task, inner fragmentation, the desire to widen one's horizons, disconnected from one's calling or environment, finding fulfillment from an inwardly focused journey.

APPENDIX

table of correspondences

❦

NAME	THE FOOL (0)				TEMPERANCE (14)
ASTRO	♅ – Uranus				♐ – Sagittarius
ELEMENT	△ – Air				△ – Fire
STONE	Turquoise, fulgurites				Jacinth, amethyst, pyrite
PLANT	Ginseng, peppermint				Echinacea, valerian
KABBALAH	א – Aleph				ס – Samech

NAME	THE MAGICIAN (1)	THE DEVIL (15)
ASTRO	☿ – Mercury	♑ – Capricorn
ELEMENT	△ – Air	△ – Earth
STONE	Citrine, Tiger Eye, quicksilver	Obsidian, jet, black diamond
PLANT	Astragalus, ginkgo, fennel	Lobelia, thistles, fig
KABBALAH	ב – Bet	ע – Ayin

NAME	THE HIGH PRIESTESS (2)	STRENGTH (8)	THE TOWER (16)
ASTRO	☽ – the Moon	♌ – Leo	♂ – Mars
ELEMENT	▽ – Water	△ – Fire	△ – Fire
STONE	Moonstone, pearl, silver	Cat's eye, chrysolite	Lodestone, garnet, iron
PLANT	Peony, artemisias, pomegranate	Cayenne, sunflower, comfrey	Garlic, absinthe, rue
KABBALAH	ג – Gimel	ט – Tet	פ – Pe

NAME	THE EMPRESS (3)	THE HERMIT (9)	THE STAR (17)
ASTRO	♀ – Venus	♍ – Virgo	♒ – Aquarius
ELEMENT	△ – Earth	△ – Earth	△ – Air
STONE	Emerald, rose quartz, copper	Peridot, bloodstone	Quartz, turquoise
PLANT	Dong quai, rose, damiana	Licorice, narcissus	Skullcap, silver fir, coconut
KABBALAH	ד – Dalet	י – Yod	צ – Tzaddi

NAME	THE EMPEROR (4)	WHEEL OF FORTUNE (10)	THE MOON (18)
ASTRO	♈ – Aries	♃ – Jupiter	♓ – Pisces
ELEMENT	△ – Fire	△ – Fire	▽ – Water
STONE	Ruby, red garnet	Amethyst, lapis lazuli, sapphire, tin	Opal, moonstone, selenite
PLANT	Atractylodes, oak, laurel	Slippery elm, dandelion, lemon balm	Lemon balm, poppy, eucalyptus
KABBALAH	ה – Hay	ק – Qof	ק – Kuo

NAME	THE HIEROPHANT (5)	JUSTICE (11)	THE SUN (19)
ASTRO	♉ – Taurus	♎ – Libra	☉ – Sun
ELEMENT	△ – Earth	△ – Air	△ – Fire
STONE	Jade, topaz	Jade, coral	Diamond, heliotrope, gold
PLANT	Sage, lavender, violet	Plantain, aloe, tobacco	Angelica, rosemary, sunflower
KABBALAH	ו – Vau	ל – Lamed	ר – Raish

NAME	THE LOVERS (6)	THE HANGED MAN (12)	JUDGEMENT (20)
ASTRO	♊ – Gemini	♆ – Neptune	♇ – Pluto
ELEMENT	△ – Air	▽ – Water	▽ – Water
STONE	Agate, alexandrite	Beryl, aquamarine	Malachite, hematite
PLANT	Parsley, dragon's blood, orchid	Kelp, water lilies, grape	Goldenseal, hibiscus, red poppy
KABBALAH	ז – Zayin	מ – Mem	ש – Shin

NAME	THE CHARIOT (7)	DEATH (13)	THE WORLD (21)
ASTRO	♋ – Cancer	♏ – Scorpio	♄ – Saturn
ELEMENT	▽ – Water	▽ – Water	△ – Earth
STONE	Amber, chalcedony	Snakestone, bloodstone	Onyx, black pearl, lead
PLANT	Cyperus, lotus	Yew, myrtle, elderflowers	Comfrey, bay laurel, hellebore
KABBALAH	ח – Chet	נ – Nun	ת – Tav